First, I thank God for allowing me the wisdom and strength throughout my life to express myself. Next, I thank all my relatives and friends here and gone on. I feel my Mom and Dads' presence daily -guiding my steps. I thank my poodles for sitting up with me when I write at 3am!

I want to thank all First Responders, Core of Engineers, Scientists, Military, Police, Laboratories, Pharmaceutical Companies, Dr Moncef Slaoui, General G. Perna, CDC Director Redfield, FDA Hahn, General Semonite, Corona Task Force, V.P. Pence, Dr. Fauci, Dr. Deborah Birx, Secretary Esper, Secretary Azar, Admiral B. Giroir, and the leader President Donald J Trump.

"COVerup ID' – 2019"

"Learning from our past allows us to avoid the pitfalls of the future."

DIANNE ANDREWS

"COVerup ID' – 2019"

EXPOSED

ISBN: 978-1-63684-445-9

Printed in Baton Rouge, Louisiana

This book is printed on acid-free paper.

First Edition

14 13 12 11 10 / 10 9 8 7 6 5 4 3 2 1

TABLE OF CONTENTS

D-Day COVID-19..1

Operation Warp Speed..9

Were the States Ready? What Was Their Response?....17

Ventilators in Record Time,
PPE in the USA 21

China, Viruses, and the World!..........................26

Therapeutics, Vaccines and
Politics Make Strange Bedfellows.......................30

Have Masks Will Travel! 35

Are Women Superior to Men When It Comes to
COVID-19 Deaths?...40

Worldwide Lockdowns
—Yes, No, Maybe???...43

Tidbits and Lagniappe..47

References/Sources...50

Appendix 52

D-DAY COVID-19

Many are reading my title and saying this has been the greatest failure for any viral response by the United States. I will ask you: What do you really know about what has been done? Just the daily death tolls and case counts? Take an hour or two and follow me on this journey. I believe you will come to agree with me—or at least come to know a lot more about our fight against this invisible enemy.

Pandemic, corona, coronavirus, novel (new) coronavirus, 2019-CoV, SARS, SARS-CoV2, COVID-19—10 months ago, we started hearing these names. At first, most of us paid no attention. Now they are part of our daily routine, in our actions, deeds, and words.

"Let me get my mask!" "I forgot my hand sanitizer!" "Those people aren't social distancing!" We hear this a lot. How easy it's become to panic! Who do I believe? It's very exhausting!

Let me be clear. This virus is no "HOAX". There is a distinct difference between a hoax and cover-ups on many levels.

With COVerup ID'-2019 we will follow the science, the administration, China, the World Health Organization (WHO), and the country. But, more importantly, I will talk about what "we the people" need to know about medicines, therapeutics, field hospitals, mask mishaps, COVID-19 death models—real or fake—the status of vaccines, and testing issues and victories.

You might ask, "Who told what to the president?" which resulted in the severe economic shutdowns and social lockdowns. This is a good question, regardless of whether in your opinion things went right or wrong-gone well or awry. Let's try to bring clarity and facts to this last 10 months of uncertainty.

On January 14, 2020, the WHO announced to the world via a press conference that the novel coronavirus had jumped from animal to human and was now resulting in human-to-human transmission. This is a process named zoonosis. A few days afterward, there were speculations that this had been known by Chinese officials and the WHO for up to eight weeks. Also there has always been a question of whether the virus was sold in a horseshoe bat at the Wuhan wet meat market or released by mistake or on purpose from the Wuhan Biosafety Level (BSL) 4 Lab of Virology means it was man made. Either way President Trump stopped all flights to and from China, on our Western border 17 days later.

In January, the CDC started monitoring five US airports (New York JFK, SF International, LA International, Chicago O'Hare, ATL Hartfield) and 20 ports, where the majority of Chinese passengers arrived into the United States. Both ports and airports had medical testing stations.

Prior to the stoppage, there were 8,000 passengers daily from China into the United States and 6,000 passengers from the United States to China—a total of 14,000 daily. That adds up to 98,000 weekly and 5,110,000 yearly. Yes over five million a year!

A few of our index cases coming in from Wuhan tested positive on January 21. The media focused mostly on the man from Seattle, Washington, who was tested then hospitalized for two weeks. Afterwards, he was COVID-19 free and returned to his life.

On January 30, the president launched a task force to monitor and prevent the spread of the novel coronavirus, headed by Secretary of Health and Human Services Alex Azar. Later VP Mike Pence led the task force. At that time, the United States had five confirmed cases, which were all on the West Coast, except one in Illinois. This includes the Seattle case. All were monitored for three days for symptoms. This comes also after 200 Americans were evacuated from Wuhan, China, which was considered the epicenter at that time—and more so now.

Who did the statistical modeling for the COVID-19 deaths? Dr Anthony Fauci, MD, director of National Institute of Allergy and Infectious Disease, and Dr. Deborah Birx, MD, Global Health Official, response coordinator for the coronavirus task force (appointed by VP Pence), who informed our president of the potential death rates, which resulted in the economic closures and social lockdowns of 42 states.

The Institute for Health Metrics and Evaluation (IHME), located at the University of Washington and Neal Ferguson's team at Imperial College London had two different death modeling estimates. One stated that the United States would probably lose up to 2.2 million people if it did not act quickly and decisively. Some believed, to lower the deaths, we should close most states' economies and initiate stay-at-home orders. It seems that the IHME model greatly overestimated hospital beds and ventilator needs.

Dr. Deborah Birx and Dr. Anthony Fauci briefed the president at the White House per Cato at Liberty, at the Cato Institute. The subject was a graph they showed on March 31, 2020, at a previous White House briefing displaying two bell-shaped epidemic curves placed on top of each other. The steeper curve was labeled "Pandemic Out" that projected 1.5 to 2.2 million deaths by June 20, 2020. The second graph labeled "With Interventions" projected 100,000 to 240,000 deaths by October 2020. This illustrates that, from both models' death numbers, the quick decisive actions and mitigation have saved lives. Dr. Fauci is on record saying that the president's actions were "impressive" and "saved lives."

Dr. Birx stated that the death rates could be at the lower 240,000 estimate "if we do things perfectly." Every life is precious! I am not saying this was a success, but we are a long way from 2.2 million! To the mother who lost her grandmother or the son who lost his father, nothing is perfect. Life cannot be measured in terms of success to them. The purpose of this book is to communicate the many actions not publicized by the mainstream media regarding what has been done to try and to save more lives. We highlight the errors in hindsight that we now know. This is like a war against an invisible enemy, the kind the world has not seen in over a hundred years. While you are in the mist of war, with limited information, do you retreat or never give up? I think this administration never gave up seeking solutions. But you be the judge.

On January 31, President Trump issued a proclamation (featured in the appendix) to close our Western border to China. Of course American citizens and some others were allowed to return to the United States. There was a military base where these travelers were quarantined using CDC protocols in California.

China stopped all flights within its borders but still flew flights with potentially viral infected people to the rest of the world. Italy and the United States stopped fights within a day of each other. In the spring, Italy had the world's highest death toll and rate. It has a population of 60 million people, with many elderly people with comorbidities. Most of Europe did not stop flights from China until the middle of March.

The president wanted to close the US Eastern border to Europe at the same time but delayed the closing until March because he was already being called a racist and xenophobe by Speaker Pelosi, who had started the impeachment hearings (for a call to Ukraine speaking briefly on VP Biden and his son Hunter on potential fraud) against the President on January 16.

On February 24, Speaker Pelosi was in Chinatown with no mask, asking Americans to come visit and saying that the situation was under control. Former VP Biden also joined in on the criticism with other Democrats. Former Bush and Obama Secretary of Defense, Dr. Robert Gates in his memoirs stated that Joe Biden had been wrong on nearly every foreign policy and national security issue over the last four decades of his almost 50 years in politics. Gates confirmed his statement again in 2019 on CBS's "Face the Nation" when asked if Biden would be a good president.

I believe this is the greatest public/private partnership mobilization in our history in a short period of time against an unknown virus. The president chose to save lives and closed the best US economy probably ever! Closing the border to China saved lives while Biden, Pelosi, Cuomo, DeBlasio, and Whitmer called him racist. Maskless Pelosi talked about coming to San Francisco Chinatown as she hugged people while NY officials were saying, "It won't be that bad."

There are so many examples of Democratic hypocrisy: Feinstein maskless getting off her private plane; Pelosi at the San Francisco salon getting her hair done, maskless; Cuomo in NY and DeBlasio out in the city seen maskless; Leslie Stahl maskless at the White House and Chris Cuomo in several places maskless; Chicago Mayor Lightfoot maskless on Facebook at her salon. After being caught, she held a press conference saying, "she had to look good." Don't we all? What hypocrites! Google all of these politicians or media in places without masks in the last several months:

Biden did not start wearing a mask until June and was doing rallies before becoming a ghost in the basement. In June, it became a campaign issue. There have been many mask mishaps!

As Governor Christy said, "I made a mistake not wearing a mask" after a serious bout with COVID-19. But this month, October, the CDC stated over 74 percent of all COVID-19 patients said they wore a mask all the time, and 14.5 percent said most of the time.

Shutting down this large an economy for any president would be a heavy decision. But people forget that no one ever had to make this decision before. No one! 1918 was a much smaller economy and more localized. Inheriting a bad economy to fix is so different than closing possibly the best one ever. Our economy was out of recession, a good one that President Trump put on steroids. Trump created this economy by reducing business-strangling regulations, making the US number one in oil production in the world, creating opportunity zones in poor areas, and reducing taxes for every American.

The ramifications were incredible, with the greatest economy for Blacks, for Hispanics, for Women, for Americans, with the lowest unemployment rate in over 50 years at 3.5 percent.

The Obama/Biden median jobless rate was 7.7 percent per Factcheck.org during their administration. At the end of their tenure, it was 7.8 percent. After the economic closure in March, the US unemployment rate rose to over 25 percent. It was 7.8 percent in October and 6.7 percent in November. This is an amazing number after the greatest economic wreck (because of China) since the Great Depression. It has only been five months and even without the entire economy open, such as in New York City, New Orleans, and Los Angeles (all Dem mayors), the economy was in an upswing. For Blacks and Browns, the median income grew by $7K in three years. Under Obama/Biden, in eight years it only grew $975.

Trump closed in on the wealth gap and lowered the poverty

rates from 20.8 percent to 18.8 percent for Blacks and 17 percent to 15.7 percent for Browns and 12 percent to 10.5 percent for the country. This is the lowest since 1959 when the US starting releasing poverty records. Wow (per Census.gov)! The rest of the world is doing much worse than the United States economically due to the virus.

Biden led one of the slowest recession recovery's ever. Even receiving almost $1 trillion in an economic stimulus package in their first year, which many forgot. Remember the automobile and Wall Street bailouts?

"Vision is to know what can be even though it's not there to see."

— *Dianne Andrews*

OPERATION WARP SPEED

President Trump took quick and decisive action following the science and the recommendations of his COVID-19 task force. However, as we have seen, following the science can be difficult because not all scientists agree.

In record time, President Trump reauthorized the Defense Production Act of 1950 from the Korean War. This spring, General Motors, Ford, and Ventec Life Systems manufactured ventilators by reopening and retooling factories in the Midwest. Honeywell and 3M both started making personal protective equipment (PPE). Most previously were made in China. Even most medicines, including 90 percent of our antibiotics, are made in China. China even threatened to halt production and distribution to the US during this pandemic. In March, companies such as BrewDog and many small breweries and distillers used their expertise to make hand sanitizers.

In July, Kodak announced it would create 300 jobs in upstate New York. It became a part of the Presidents' Defense Production Act to produce pharmaceuticals for generic COVID-19 drugs. Plus, many stand-alone small households became entrepreneurs to make PPE.

On April 17, Army Lt. Gen. Todd Semonite, commander of the Army Corps of Engineers, implemented enormous field hospital implementation projects. The complete story can be found on the Department of Defense, DOD News.

The Corps completed the New York City Jacob Javits Convention Center upgrade to a 3,000-bed field hospital in a matter of weeks. His team of 36,000 employees, of which 99.5 percent were civilians, worked 18 to 19 hours a day with the full thanks and support of the president and the DOD, FEMA, and HHS. They built 28 alternate care facilities in

20 states, supplying 15,800 beds for COVID-19 patients. Additionally, 11 requests came in the first weeks of April.

This temporary hospital facilities was designed to relieve stress on overcrowded hospitals. After all, we needed to flatten the curve in maybe two to four weeks. Right? Some other centers included the Denver Convention Center; St. Louis Convention Center; Washington, DC Convention Center; and ones in New Jersey, New Orleans, and Chicago. They also converted hotels and dormitories into hospitals.

Commander Semonite said his first objective was the safety of his people. PPE was supplied, temperature checks were given, and social distancing was possible. He supplied a turnkey design blueprint to governors of 41 states. This allowed the states to build these facilities at the state level. This was a nonstandard solution, but the Corps rose to the occasion and provided it in record time.

Additionally, the president sent two 1,000-bed Navy hospital ships with 12 operating rooms, the size of three football fields—10 stories high. Both the Mercy and Comfort were deployed to Los Angeles and New York City, respectively. They were to be for patients with life-threatening needs and emergency surgeries, allowing the main hospitals to care for COVID-19 patients.

On April 27, the Comfort, after a three-and-a-half-week stint in New York City, only treating 182 patients but spending millions, returned home to Norfolk, Virginia, with only 18.2 percent utilization. Even during the virus's peak! Because of all the temporary hospitals and ventilator requests, and a lot of overestimation by Governor Cuomo and other governors, the underutilization was amazing. However, on April 13, Cuomo stated, "Trump has delivered for NY." A similar situation occurred in Los Angeles, with the Mercy and

Governor Newsom. Models again overestimated the need for ventilators and hospital beds. The point is that our president sent them everything requested. Cuomo was complimentary then, but not now, as almost 7,000 nursing home patients died under his watch. Governor Newsom praised Trump as California awaited coronavirus supplies.

On May 15, the DHHS and DOD under Operation Warp Speed (OWS) partnered to work with private industry with the goal of delivering safe and effective doses of COVID-19 vaccines by year end. Four pharmaceutical companies have gone into phase 3 trials under OWS: Johnson & Johnson, Moderna, AstraZeneca, and Pfizer. This in magnitude and size is an unprecedented effort. The COVID-19 vaccine is a two-shot system. After the first dose, the second must be taken 21 to 28 days later. There are 330 million people in America, meaning 640 million doses are needed just for the United States. In the world, there are 7.8 billion people, meaning 15.6 billion, adjusting for 5–15 percent spillage and waste, which equals 15.8 billion doses. These are really big numbers, meaning a really big job needs to be done.

The OWS scientific head is Dr. Moncef Slaoui, an immunologist who has led the successful development of 14 vaccines and is a former pharmaceutical executive. Army Gen. Gustave Perna is the CEO, along with Secretary Azar and Secretary Mike Esper. "I think it will be a very effective vaccine. That's my prediction," Slaoui said. "My personal opinion, based on my experience and the biology of this virus, I think this vaccine is going to be highly efficacious."

"OWS has and continues to organize multiple, parallel lines of effort," Perna said during his Senate confirmation hearing in June. "Vaccine, therapeutics and diagnostic developments or evaluations are taking place concurrently." The HHS and DOD have already started to increase manufacturing and distribution capacity and capability. Many believe that OWS will shorten the pandemic by years.

Upon approval from the Food and Drug Administration, OWS will immediately energize manufacturing and distribution networks, in conjunction with industry partners, to speed delivery of these new products to the nation. This is the considered risk we must evaluate and be prepared to take, expanding manufacturing prior to FDA approval—as Pfizer has done. This is something that Trump wanted to do. This has not short cut science and safety. As other vaccines have waited and people died.

The Democratic ticket has put doubt in people's minds regarding vaccine safety, especially the minority community, who still feel scars from the terrible Tuskegee Syphilis Study at the Tuskegee Institute. Where some Black men even with the disease were untreated and told they were being treated for bad blood. Biden called this the Trump vaccine in a negative implication. As the VP candidate, Harris is a minority, and being less than positive on this vaccine could scare some in minority communities. These are some of the most ethical companies in the world with quality regulations!

"Both industry and our government's supporting agencies, resourcing and execution processes must also move at Warp Speed for success; I will have to ensure that our collective bureaucracies do not distract us from winning," said Army Gen. Gustave F. Perna.

The problem maybe at the state level with potential levels of incompetence and disorganization within bureaucracies that has been sometimes displayed -as the stimulus checks distribution and the nursing home deaths. Decentralization could also be an issue. Hospital delivering the vaccines with Warp Speed maybe a challenge as the vaccine maybe issued to other than the first responders and elderly in nursing homes.

"COVerup ID'–2019"

Some political candidates have called it absurd to call this the Trump vaccine. However, he is a director who gets things done. These are the people who accomplish their mission for the world. The process and people behind this are highly qualified. It is an insult to their careers, as well as our FDA and CDC.

In June, the Trump Administration extended its testing locations partnership for citizens convenience to Rite-Aid, Walgreens, Walmart, Kroger, and CVS, plus all the clinics and hospitals. Many are drive-thru testing sites located in vulnerable communities.

There have been testing issues with our CDC to say the least. So, let's discuss what happened. The first test kits were faulty, and the red tape prevented other labs from creating their own PCR tests, which is a known established technology that has been around for 35 years. All PCR testing had to be sent to the CDC in Atlanta. This caused a major slowdown—and a plethora of problems.

By February 29, the world-renowned CDC had to change its policies, and in the first week in March, it conducted 400K tests through an "accelerated policy" that achieved more rapid testing by allowing academic hospitals and commercial labs capable of performing high-quality testing to develop and use their own tests.

The administration looked again to private partnerships, to work in parallel with the government in improving testing and shortening results waiting times. Many infected people are asymptomatic and pre-symptomatic. However, these results may be less accurate than PCR testing, which requires health-care personnel. Private–public partnerships have resulted in the creation of many testing sites and rapid testing kits, such as Abbott Labs' 15-minute self-administered test.

Trump authorized 150 million of the tests to be administered free to our most vulnerable, including nursing homes, senior communities, schools, and minority communities. Theses kits were delivered to many states in October. Florida Governor Ron DeSantis said he delivered some to senior communities and watched them get results in the first week of October. It is obvious with all these partnerships that the president found a way to cut through governmental bureaucracy to get the job done and save more American lives—not even knowing that his work may have saved his own life when he contracted the virus. Also, working with the CDC and FDA cut time in getting qualified therapeutics to patients under the Emergency Use Authorization and Compassionate Use Authorization under OWS.

Rapid testing will become a global $15 billion industry, including companies such as LabCorp, Quest Diagnostics, GenBody, and many more. This industry is expected to be reduced significantly by 2024, with global population vaccinations being projected to be completed by 2023. Dr. Fauci has said that, by April 2021, US first responders could be vaccinated, but the CDC believes it will start with first responders this year, especially with Pfizer in manufacturing currently.

Today, the United States has administered more testing than any country except China—if we can believe their numbers. But China has a population of over 1.4 billion. The United States is just 330 million. The below testing data comes from Statista.

"COVerup ID'–2019"

Test by Country as of October 10	Population
China - 160 million	1.4 billion
USA - 115 million	330 million
India - 84.6 million	1.4 billion
Russia - 49.6 million	144 million
United Kingdom - 26.7 million	66 million
Germany - 18.1 million	83 million
Brazil - 17.9 million	209 million
Spain - 13.6 million	47 million
Italy - 12 million	60 million

Also, per capita, we have performed more tests. Many countries only test when the patient exhibits signs of the virus not prior to them being sick, as the United States does pretesting. This is why we have so many cases because of the preemptive testing—done without people having to exhibit signs. More tests can bring down our fatality rate if you just divide the number of cases into number of deaths.

The United States and other countries offered to send scientists to China to assist in COVID-19 analysis in February, but the offer was declined. As we know, China was not forthcoming on viral transmission to humans, not telling us until the middle of January, which is believed to have cost hundreds of thousands of lives around the world. Africa allowed the last administration to send medical teams into the countries for assistance- with West Africa allowing the United States to assist with teams on Ebola and Zika, unlike China.

"Challenges are the ways life puts us through tests that bring out our best."

— *Dianne Andrews*

WERE THE STATES READY? WHAT WAS THEIR RESPONSE?

NY Gov. Cuomo said, regarding the Coronavirus, "No need to panic or close down mass transit as China has done. We're really trying to protect the vulnerable populations for whom the virus could really be dangerous, including senior citizens and the immune compromised. It is really in Westchester where you have a cluster of cases." This was in his interview on FNC's Sunday Morning Futures. Is it not strange that New York has been and continues to have the highest death rates in the country, especially with the vulnerable in nursing homes? New York is not our largest state. It is the fourth-largest by population, but it leads the country by almost double in deaths. Texas has more people, with fewer deaths, and California has 40 million people, and about the same number of deaths as Texas and Florida. Moreover, New Jersey, with only 8.9 million residents, has a very high number of nursing home deaths.

In August, four states accounted for 65 percent of the total US deaths: New York, Pennsylvania, Massachusetts, and New Jersey—with over 50 percent from nursing homes. By September, there were almost 7,000 nursing home deaths in New Jersey. Massachusetts had over 64 percent of their deaths in long-term care homes, and 18 states have over half of their deaths in nursing and veteran homes. One soldiers' home in Massachusetts had 76 COVID-19 deaths!

Nursing and veteran homes are state run, managed under a license, and inspected by the state. These deaths would not be patients walking around outside. I owned a geriatric home health and also hosted television shows with experts on viruses, epidemics, and pandemics. Today, 40 percent of all COVID-19 deaths are in long-term care facilities. Midsummer, it was 59 percent in state-controlled long-term care homes. These people were not walking around in public without masks, spreading the virus or in our now closed houses of worship. Maybe they were at the opened casinos!?

The CDC has stated COVID-19 is a highly contagious disease. On my television show I spoke with an infectious disease MD on the virus mutation. One new strain is reported in Europe and is thought to be highly contagious strain but no more deadly.

Out of those over 75 years of age, 95 percent survive. In those less than 50 years old, 99.1 percent survive. Hospitalizations and death rates are down by 40percent in the country, as of October, though cases again are up. (In COVerup-ID' 2019, I show you deaths by states and testing numbers by country).

Should we hold the governors accountable for these state-run venues accounting for 80K US deaths? These were patients that were not spreading the disease in the environment. Let's subtract those 80K from the total, bringing the number down to 137K from 217K deaths. Should the states be blamed? Definitely look at their processes. For more info, read the Bill of Health on September 9, by James Lytle, plus other articles on New Jersey's handling of COVID-19 in long-term care homes.

In September, per the CDC, 94 percent of all COVID-19 deaths had 2.5 other serious diseases or comorbidities. These include high blood pressure, obesity, diabetes, COPD, cardiovascular disease including heart disease, kidney disease, cancer or being a cancer survivor, and immune deficiency. Only 6 percent or 10K cases were COVID-19 only deaths, which means no comorbidities were associated with these deaths. For elderly patients with severe diseases, which was the chicken and which was the egg? What was the true cause you may question? However, for a family of a loved one at 100, it is a tragedy!

We often forget that this is a worldwide pandemic, a disease outbreak that spread across multiple countries with many cases. COVID-19 has resulted in cases in over 215 countries to be exact. Where an epidemic is an outbreak of increased infections in a regional area, a pandemic involves outbreaks in many countries.

Below are deaths and population rates for states with the highest death tolls in the United States, as of October 10, 2020. All deaths are a tragedy! Louisiana, my state, has what seems one of the highest per capita death rates. Most believe this is because of Mardi Gras. This makes sense because millions of people from all over the world come to a small area with no mitigation requirements. I knew about the virus in February. I was planning shows with our state epidemiologist. My first was in March. I gloved up, masked, and sterilized my building and social distanced guests.

I wonder why our public servants did not give out that criteria?

Death Totals from Statista (as of October 10, 2020)

Deaths	Population
New York - 33K	19.4 million
Texas - 16.7K	29 million
California - 16.4K	40 million
New Jersey - 16K	8.9 million
Florida - 15K	21.5 million
MASS - 9.5K	6.9 million
Illinois - 9.1K	12.7 million
PA - 8.2K	12.8 million
Georgia - 7.2K	10.6 million
Michigan - 7.2K	9.9 million
Arizona - 5.7K	7.3 million
Louisiana - 5.6K	4.7 million
Ohio - 4.9K	11.7 million

"Changing attitudes leads to the path of changing minds."

—Dianne Andrews

VENTILATORS IN RECORD TIME, PPE IN THE USA

The president has said no one died for lack of a ventilator and has aided other countries by ensuring they could acquire them from us, even free. He said this was not about money but saving lives. Again, many state and national models were way off base on requirements and actual needs.

The president's son-in-law, Jared Kushner, a senior administration advisor, was an integral liaison with the states on the ventilator project. Some governors complimented him for assisting them in getting correct ventilator requirements, as opposed to some state and national model numbers. He raised his status with critics when he did an excellent job in the Middle East peace talks, resulting in peace deals called the "Trump Doctrine" for which the president has been nominated for three Nobel Peace Prizes.

The national PPE N95s supply was depleted and never replenished by the last administration, and they were warned of that fact. The ventilator numbers, per the experts, did fall short of what would be needed in a pandemic. Per Snopes, budget figures show that, in 2013, stockpile funding dropped to its lowest level of $477 million under Obama/Biden. Today the budget is $705 million.

What about our states' supplies? Seems many states were MIA on their own watches. NY Governor Cuomo, in 2015, per the New York Times (October 25, 2015), invested $750 million in a failed attempt to move a solar panel company called Solar City out of California to Buffalo. This was his largest state-funded economic development project. Some think that could have gone for a ventilator supply (per Bristol Herald Courier).

By the end of May 2020, Panasonic was to cease US solar manufacturing operations in Buffalo and is scheduled to exit the facility by the end of September 2020 (as stated by the Democrat and Chronicle on February 26, 2020).

Remember Solyndra, the solar panel company that went under in 2011 from the Obama/Biden Administration and defaulted on a $535 million loan guarantee, taxpayer money, from the Department of Energy? Guess what! Solar City went into that same building, leasing 200,000 sq ft.

Also, a 2008 study (Cuomo was not in office) and the 2015 Ventilator Allocation Guidelines Commissioned under the governor suggests lottery color coding ventilator usage by severity of sickness based on certain criteria. Some call this death panel decisions.

During the early months of this pandemic, the governor is said to have told officials to keep nursing home patients in their nursing homes without ventilators or proper supplies for survival. This has always baffled me when hosting COVID-19 shows discussing the deaths on my television show Dianne Andrews in Black & White (www.youtube.com/dianneandrewsshow), interviewing doctors and respiratory therapists—from epidemiologists to psychologists to infectious disease doctors to pulmonologists to family practitioners. One of the MDs I interviewed survived the disease during this pandemic.

Overall, 90 percent of our country's PPE was being manufactured and imported from—YOU GUESSED IT—China. During this pandemic, there were some hints that China made threats to stop sending needed supplies and medicines to the United States.

US Senator Lindsey Graham (R-South Carolina) developed legislation to provide tax credits and incentives to move the production of PPE from China back to the United States

PPE is a critical national security need for doctors, nurses, and health-care providers fighting COVID-19. PPE can consist of clothing, sanitizing supplies, ancillary medical supplies (wipes, bedding, test swabs, etc.), gloves, and masks. Senator Graham's plan would establish a $7.5 billion medical manufacturing project tax credit to build out and retrofit factories to meet increased PPE demand here and give US businesses incentives (lgraham.senate.gov).

One of this administration's slogan has always been, "Bring it back and make it here." Of course "Make America Great Again" is the best known. This is survival, not isolation. Japan announced in April it would be taking control of its PPE supply chain, taking it back from China, putting billions into their businesses to produce it in Japan (Article in Forbes).

The supply chain will never be the same. Take that to the bank literally!

It's not Donald (called the "Tariff Man") Trump's fault anymore. It's COVID-19's fault for shaking things up. The geopolitical watchdogs at the Spectator Index noted that Japan's government would spend upwards of $2 billion helping its multinationals leave China. Japan's decision to help companies source elsewhere, a timely and expensive endeavor after multinational corporations have made China their go-to manufacturing hub for decades, comes at a time when US companies are leaving.

All humans want control of their destinies. And why shouldn't countries? Let's not forget this is the Chinese Communist Party, which is worth $14.1 trillion. Our GDP is $21.4 trillion, and Russia is not even $2 trillion. But in terms of purchasing power, the United States loses its #1 spot to China (per Investopedia).

Biden said, "China is no competition." I beg to differ. Who is really the one after us? I think China is saying it will lead the world's economy in a short time. They are building Navy in the world. But we know this is only with help from some powerful, greedy Americans selling us out. Maybe many of our politicians. And billionaires who have multiple businesses in China!

"Evil lurks in the hearts of plenty, make sure to protect yourself to survive the attacks of many."

—*Dianne Andrews*

China, Viruses, and the World!

Let's discuss China's only biological security level four-certified lab, where this horseshoe bat meat may have escaped to the nearby "zoo" meat market—whether by mistake or on purpose. Either way, it is the Wuhan virus!

Dr. Li Meng Yan is a Chinese virologist who escaped from China in April 2020 to America. She risked her own life to tell the world the truth about COVID-19. Her mother has been jailed because of Yan's desire to warn the world that China purposefully did this to the world on two levels (1) as a bioweapon and (2) holding the truth too long that this was a human-to-human transmissible virus. The WHO did not announce this to the world until January 14. This life-saving fact was known to them at least six weeks earlier!

All adults usually are exposed to coronaviruses. The most common one is, yes, the common cold. This virus group looks like a crown under the microscope, thus the name "corona" (which means crown in Latin). In the beginning of the outbreak, many believed the disease came from the Corona beer. This is laughable today. But not then. People were so afraid and panicking.

Wikipedia states that the cold was ID'ed in the 1950s. Others believe it has been around since early history. Science Daily has an article from the Society of General Microbiology stating that the common cold originated in birds then jumped to humans 200 years ago. As we have mentioned earlier this process is called zoonosis. Many viruses come from bats. There is usually an intermediary, which is many times a civet cat. There have also been pigs, camels, and other intermediaries, prior to jumping to humans.

Sometimes the cure can be worse than the disease, but a global panic is always the worst of all. The novel coronavirus or SAR-CoV2, resulting in COVID-19, is the only coronavirus that has resulted in a pandemic. Some have been epidemics but not world wide pandemics.

There were only two previous pandemics in the 21st century: The Swine flu H1N1/09 was indexed in April 2009, believed to have come from a pig in Mexico and declared a pandemic in June 2009. The WHO declared an end to the pandemic in August 2010—but not before it infected 60 million people. Yes, we had 60 million cases and 12K deaths in the United States. H1N1 killed globally over 57K people in 213 countries.

Ronald Klain, chief of staff for VP Joe Biden, said in 2019, "It is purely fortuitous that this was not one of the great mass casualty events in American history. It had nothing to do with us doing anything right. It just had to do with luck." Politico interviewed two dozen people from the administration to Congress and outsiders who described a litany of obstacles, vaccine creation shortfalls, and contradictory messaging.

Probably the mostly deadly respiratory virus in history is the influenza virus, which caused the Spanish flu of 1918. The flu is not in the coronavirus family. Some estimates believe that, from 1918 thru 1919, the Spanish flu killed 50 to 100 million people. Although reporting was not as good as today, there were 500 million cases reported, which was half the world population at that time. This virus did not just index in Spain but the whole world. We call it the Spanish flu because Spain had a free press during the war and was one of the only countries that reported on the virus openly. Because of the virus contagion, World War I troop movements were believed to be the main factors in its rapid worldwide transmission. President Woodrow Wilson contracted the flu in 1919 and almost died while in Paris conducting peace talks.

Still today the influenza virus kills from 35,000 to 80,000 people, depending on the year. And pneumonia kills 50,000 yearly—both with a vaccine and some herd immunity! Per the

CDC, last year the flu killed 188 children younger than 18. COVID-19 took 121 lives younger than 21 years old in 2020.

Just to put deadly diseases into perspective: lung cancer kills 170,000 yearly, and 150,000 are preventable deaths linked to cigarette smoking. Cancer is the second leading cause of death in the United States. Total deaths are 588,274, with more deaths in men. The leading cause of death in the United States is heart disease at 655,000, again more in men, with one person dying every 36 seconds from cardiovascular disease.

Many viruses do carry the name of the index area such as Ebola (from bats), Zika from (Aedes mosquitos), both from regions in Africa. In 2012, a coronavirus, the Middle East Respiratory Syndrome, originated in Saudi Arabia. It was transmitted by a bat to a camel to humans. In 2002, the world faced the Severe Acute Respiratory Syndrome (SARS), the cousin to SARS-CoV2. Again, this came from bats and from China. Neither MERS nor SARS outbreaks resulted in pandemics, and there were no vaccines created. SARS went away after almost two years. It was found 29 countries, including the United States during that period.

Similarly, to Woodrow Wilson, President Donald Trump contracted COVID-19 while working for the American people in September 2020. President Trump said, "I can't hide in a basement. I'm running a country. Now I'm immune! I'm going to make Regeneron available to every citizen that needs it FREE!" Dr. Ben Carson was supplied it by the President request for him to the MD and recovered in 3 days after receiving it.

"From seeds of discipline sprout the roots of leadership."

—Dianne Andrews

THERAPEUTICS, VACCINES AND POLITICS MAKE STRANGE BEDFELLOWS.

What was the president's medication regime? Was it just for him or ALL Americans?

His treatment was very similar to an average COVID-19 patient. All his prescribed drugs and OTC are available for all patients if their MD deems them useful for their COVID-19 recovery. The president is working through the red tape on getting Regeneron free to all whose physicians believe it can aid in the patients' progress. The normal cost will be $2,000 per dose. It consists of two antibodies—one from a recovered COVID-19 patient and the other from a synthetic antibody of a mouse engineered to have a human immune system. It reduces viral load and improves patient conditions. This drug can be given outside the hospital setting. One intravenous transfusion lasts up to four months.

Regeneron received $450 million in government funding in July 2020 as part of the president's OWS initiative for quick vaccine development and therapeutics. Human trials began in June with 275 in the first phase. Eli Lily has a similar antibody cocktail. The two companies are slated to produce one million doses for the American people. Regeneron was given to our president under a Compassionate Use Authorization from the FDA requested by Dr. Sean Conley.

Little did President Trump know his commitment to the American people on this virus would save his own life! This is a true testament to our president and all who led on this virus!

Dr. Conley is a DO (osteopathic doctor) not an MD (allopathic doctor). The DO course of study is very similar to MD clinical pathways, which is different here than in Europe.

DO processes work in a holistic approach to medicine. They represent 11 percent of current US physicians and comprise 20 percent of current medical students.

President Trump's medication regime also included Remdesivir, which was the first therapeutic authorized in May for COVID-19. The cost is $2,340 to $3,120. It is an antiviral administered by IV. It has been under development since 2009, according to Gilead, the manufacturer. Dr Fauci, the NIAID director who has a budget of $5.9 billion this year, was instrumental in the Emergency Use Authorization for this drug. Public Citizen has stated that taxpayers contributed at least $70.5 million to develop this drug, working with the NIAID. Originally for Hep C, Ebola, SARS, MERS, and two other coronaviruses, it was first developed under the Obama/Biden Administration and used in Ebola treatment. But it did not prove to assist in reducing death rates. Trials purportedly showed it could accelerate recovery time by up to four or five days. There is some concern from the WHO currently regarding its effectiveness—even though the FDA authorized it as a COVID-19 treatment in October.

Dexamethasone is a common steroid believed to reduce COVID-19 deaths by up to one-third of hospitalized patients. Per the Mayo Clinic, this drug provides relief for inflammation. It is usually used in severe cases to reduce lung inflammation. Its cost is only $25.

The rest of President Trump's medication regime included OTC drugs: zinc, vitamin D, famotidine (the medication in Pepcid for heartburn or acid reflux), melatonin, and a daily aspirin. President Trump's age, weight, and gender all placed him at higher risk for severe coronavirus illness. He does lead a drug and alcohol free lifestyle. His recovery was thus miraculous! Trump revealed he had COVID-19 on October 2 and was admitted and stayed in the Walter Reed National

Military Medical Center for only three days. It was reported that he was COVID-19 free on October 9 by Dr. Conley and his medical team.

At the University of Buffalo, Thomas Russo conducted one study (there are more) showing that patients were found to be 20 times more likely to have been infected indoors than outdoors. Vitamin D deficiency is important for bone, muscle and teeth. But several studies have shown that a deficiency may influence the risk and severity of this infection.

One of the president's therapeutics was vitamin D. Vitamin D is different from some other vitamins because it is produced when our largest organ, the skin, is exposed to the sun. It is called the "sunshine vitamin." Only about 10 percent of it comes from our diets. Scientists are researching the vitamin, as our immune cells have vitamin D receptors. Right now, people are spending more time indoors due to stay-in restrictions, so this could be a problem with community spread. Since it is the largest percentage of the infection.

There Are Two Other Therapeutics That the President Took Heat For

One is Pulmotect, a bio-pharmaceutical company out of Houston, Texas, working at MD Anderson and Texas A&M. This company develops products to reduce morbidity and mortality in patients at risk of severe respiratory diseases. Its product PUL-42 is an aerosol inhaled therapeutic that stimulates the innate immunity in the lungs. It is like cleaning the virus from the lungs, which, as a non-clinician, the president asked his clinical team about. This seems to be what he was mentioning. There have been two clinical trials. It has been tested on mice and in limited human trials. The company believes it is less than a year away from FDA approval.

The second being hydroxychloroquine which is a drug used to treat for malaria, lupus and rheumatoid arthritis. Some scientists believe it alleviates COVID-19. The president took this during the summer, probably along with azithromycin and zinc—the three-pack used as a preventative. Per his team, he experienced no side effects to his heart, which was one of the FDA warnings. Henry Ford Hospital in Detroit also did a 2,541-patient study, which some say showed positive results for the drug. But the FDA disagreed on its merits for this virus. Many doctors swear by it, but some studies show it to be ineffective. Black Detroit State Representative Karen Whitsett said she felt better within a few hours of taking the prescription. She went to the White House to thank the president, which upset her Democratic leaders. But she believed saving her life deserved a thank you. She and her doctor said it did save her life. Thus, you should follow your MD's advice.

"Success at its best is you passing all life's tests."

—*Dianne Andrews*

HAVE MASKS WILL TRAVEL!

In October, a new CDC study found the majority of those infected with COVID-19 "always" wore masks (74 percent) or most of the time (14.5 percent). Maskne is acne or other skin irritations around the mouth and face that results from wearing an N-95, surgical, or cloth mask. Prior to COVID-19, it was not really mentioned, but it started to trend during this pandemic because of the widespread mask usage. It turns out that most mask wearers still contracted COVID-19, according to a recently published study by the CDC on CDC.com. The study shows 88.5 percent of COVID-19 patients wore masks all or most of the time. Once again, it appears there are conflicting facts, data, and plenty of opinions about the efficacy of wearing masks to prevent COVID-19.

It is difficult not to conclude that wearing nonsurgical cloth face masks or face coverings has had different results and resulted in differing scientific viewpoints. On MSNBC, I saw Governor Newsom in April speaking on his decision to purchase $1 billion N95s—but from China. We are producing them here, so why China? Maybe it was timing. He purchased them from BYD, the Chinese electric car company. We see that Biden just announced, if elected, he will have a half million electric car charging stations.

I think most people do not even get it. That means no gas cars. On my television show, we just hosted a series with Democrat and Republican financial experts saying that solar panels makes us dependent on China for precious metal component in the solar panel. And eliminating fossil fuels, which includes natural gas, coal, and oil, where the United States is not the major offender. Guess who is? Again, China. The experts said there will be major economic and job losses with Biden's agenda.

Back to the masks, a CDC study, conducted by 11 medical institutions, said, the "CDC and other public health authorities recommend community mitigation strategies including social distancing to reduce transmission of SARS-CoV-2, the virus that causes COVID-19."

The CDC still recommends masks, saying "cloth face coverings help prevent people who have COVID-19 from spreading the virus to others," especially if unable to socially distance, many experts say. In December they changed to state that mask wearing also protects the wearer. Now their policy is to wear masks even with social distancing.

I hosted shows (www.youtube.com/dianneandrewsshow) with an infectious disease MD in July. We stated that mask effectiveness DEPENDS on what kind of mask. If not using N95, which is 95 percent effective against viruses. The rectangle shaped surgical mask is less effective than the N95. After that masks efficacy goes downhill quickly. Healthline has a site that shows how to make effective masks, plus many others, who sometimes disagree on filters. Follow the science. Right!

This is probably a lot of food for thought for all who don't wear one as often as they should. But, again, all data does not pan this out!

When I hosted my first COVID-19 show (www.youtube.com/dianneandrewsshow) on March 20, 2020, speaking with the Louisiana State Epidemiologist Dr. Ratard via phone and on air with the former Louisiana Asst. State Epidemiologist, they believed that masks in the summer could cause some harm because putting them on wrong or in times of too much heat could breed bacteria and cause breathing issues. Plus everyone, including Surgeon General Adams, stated "no masks" because they were needed for first responders. He now suggests for us to wear masks.

During the swine flu pandemic, the N95s were depleted and never replenished by the Obama/Biden team. Per science, our best protection from viruses is the N95. Since 88.5 percent of all infected persons wore a mask all or most of the time, either they used the wrong kind of mask, wore them wrong or this virus can penetrate through the supposedly effective masks. Who knows?

Follow the science, many say, but which one which way? Back seat drivers running for our nation's top office created a COVID-19 plan after a six-month implementation by this administration. Their plan looked very similar. It looks like plagiarism again! In the early months of the virus, scientists were giving different opinions, and the jury is still out on some.

Many states fine you monetarily if you don't wear a mask in public. But they don't ensure that the mask being worn is the best type. Many masks match some politicians and celebrities' silk dresses, ties, and knit suits, without a correct filter or multiple layers. Those masks are probably doing very little good against any virus. Below is some information on masking up for life!

I agree we should wear a mask, but we must ensure it is an effective one that is worn properly.

Mask up and Head out! Social Distance as You Can!

Before you go out in your mask, please ensure that you do the following:

-Wash your hands prior to securing your mask

-Ensure it is properly secured using ear loops or ties

-Ensure it has a snug yet comfortable fit

-Make sure you can breathe without difficulty

-Ensure it is made up of at least two layers of fabric. Many experts suggest a HEPA or coffee filter, even TED hoses. But some other experts do not (Do your research)

-Try to avoid touching your mask while you are wearing it. You see many masks unsecure and people like Speaker Pelosi pulling her matching masks up/down often. This is not good.

There are many websites on making face mask sewing or using a glue gun. Healthline has a lot of information. When removing your mask, do the following:

-Clean your hands or use hand sanitizer

-Remove the mask using the loops or ties. Don't touch the front

-Avoid touching your mouth, nose, or eyes

-Wash your hands after you take your mask off

The CDC is suggesting any child over 2 years of age must wear a mask in public. The WHO and UNICEF suggest children aged 12 and over wear masks if social distancing is not possible.

"Fear stands at the back side of courage."

—Dianne Andrews

Are Women Superior to Men When It Comes to COVID-19 Deaths?

The CDC has not kept great data on deaths by gender for this virus, but cities like New York with their total deaths are proving men are dying at higher rates than women—particularly minority men, especially those Black and Hispanic. In New York, at one time, men's deaths doubled women's. Overall, 10 women die for every 12 men. Let's examine why this may be happening.

From my geriatric health care work, interviews, and investigations, I know women's immune systems are stronger (because of the extra X chromosome) than men. This results in a stronger response to infections. Moreover, 35 percent of women are obese, as opposed to 37 percent of men. Obesity is a comorbidity for COVID-19. Heart disease is more prevalent in elderly men, along with high blood pressure and liver disease. All these comorbidities contribute to poor COVID-19 outcomes.

Another major factor arises from a study done on May 10 that reported men have higher levels of angiotensin converting enzyme (ACE2) in their blood. This allows the virus to infect healthy cells. This is a major factor for male vulnerability. There are multiple studies on these issues currently.

Environmental factors also contribute to the problem. The WHO estimates that air pollution kills more than four million people yearly through asthma, bronchitis, emphysema, lung and heart diseases, and respiratory allergies. Some believe that, because men work outdoors at higher rates than woman, this could be a factor.

Men also are less likely to see a physician as quickly. Men want to be the stronger sex, and they play that role. On my television show, in my COVID-19 series, we discussed this with a board-certified family practice physician who had had the virus and treated many elderly minority patients. Some recovered; others did not, sadly. I remember one of her patients did not want to bring his elderly mother to the hospital the night she got sick because he did not want to leave her in the hospital alone. The next day, she was hospitalized immediately. Another man did not want his test results and went to work anyway, calling later.

Even with the Spanish flu, men died at higher levels. At that time, men had higher rates of lung-damaging tuberculosis. More men also died from SARS, COVID's earlier cousin.

"Failures are your successes reversed in the mirror."

—Dianne Andrews

WORLDWIDE LOCKDOWNS
—YES, NO, MAYBE???

Do we always save the best for last? Maybe, in my case, I have saved the dreaded unknown! The WHO recently warned that lockdowns accomplish one thing—that is, making the poor poorer. It is estimated that 60 million people will be pushed into extreme poverty worldwide because of lockdowns.

VP Joe Biden has stated he will introduce lockdowns again. On 60 Minutes, in October, Dr. Fauci, who is 75 with hypertension, said in his interview that he is not ready for a national lockdown. Also, he is voting in person this year. He said that he was not surprised when the president contacted the disease, especially seeing the Rose Garden event in introducing Amy Coney Barnett for the Supreme Court, without mitigation. Again most COVID+ Americans did wear masks.

Let's look at some world experts' opinions on lockdowns. Many experts tend to believe that lockdowns only delay the virus. That it has a cycle. Is the cure worse than the disease?

John Ioannidis, a scientist from Stanford University, along with eight other world-renowned scientists, one a Nobel laureate, did not believe that the first lockdown was scientifically valid. They knew it would return until we get to over 60% to 80% herd immunity. However, some scientists believe their work is flawed.

They believe, from their studies, that the lockdown results were worse than the gain of the virus slowdown because the virus greatly affects only a small vulnerable group—per the CDC, 80 percent all deaths were for people 65 and older. In March, John emailed the administration with their advice. They believe this may have contributed to the April 15 date to reopen, as stated by the president. Although this did not happen in most states. There was never a 50-state lockdown mandate from our leader.

University of Toronto team leader Rabail Chaudhry studied 50 countries, showing that, with high obesity rates and older populations, the death rates were higher. This is similar to the United States. Additionally, countries that closed borders with full lockdowns had about the same mortality rates.

Andrew Atkeson of UCLA, with his fellow economists, found, in 23 countries and 25 US states with varying lockdown policies, the mortality rates were similar once the disease took hold. Daily deaths rose for 20 to 30 days, then fell quickly.

In Europe, Simon Wood of the University of Edinburgh concluded that infections in Britain were already declining prior to lockdowns in late March. In Germany, Thomas Wieland of the Karlsruhe Institute of Technology said that NYC is trending the same way. Studies showed COVID-19 deaths usually occurred 21 to 26 days after infection.

I discussed this with doctors on "Dianne Andrews in Black & White." Therefore, in New York, the great number of infections probably happened prior to lockdowns, with peak deaths on April 7 and lockdowns occurring on March 22. Five days prior would be March 17 for the infections.

Sweden did not go into lockdown and had an outbreak. But now their death rate is lower than many European countries. Admittedly, they floundered with nursing home response in the early days.

Lockdowns are also attributed to increased drug overdoses: March 18 percent, April 29 percent, and May 42 percent—many among younger individuals.

Suicide calls to the agencies' lines have increased by 1,000 percent, and suicide rates increased, especially among veterans and teenagers. Suicide is already the 10th-leading death cause, with up to 48K yearly deaths. For ages 10 to 23, that number is 7K. I hosted a show with a suicideologist about three years ago. There are only four in the nation. During this pandemic, the attempts considered with teens have gone from 1 in 10 to 1 in 5 teenager, per the CDC. Attempts have doubled.

Studies done on the effects of COVID-19 show 65 percent of persons were afraid of the contagion and lifestyle losses. Anxiety, insomnia, depression, and distress can lead to increased adverse life effects, such as suicide, domestic violence, and more. I discussed this with a psychologist on the show in August.

In closing, I hope this read taught you a few things. There have been eight million cases and 217K deaths in the United States, as well as 40 million cases worldwide and 1.17 million deaths. This is not a pretty picture. But I hope you can see the courses of action have saved many. Who should you listen to in a difficult crisis at a time when nothing is known? Of course, your team!

I will leave you with this: I have friends who live in Mexico and Baton Rouge who won't go back there, saying people are dying like flies, and there is no death count kept. Hospitals are horrible!

The same problems can be found in socialistic/Marxist countries, such as Cuba, China, Honduras, and Venezuela. Can we believe the world death numbers?

As you can see, you cannot just follow just the science. So many good scientists have different scientific hypotheses and theories. Who knows best? Looks like our president choose wisely! America is leading the world in the economic recovery, as well as with effective therapeutics. Dispensing is state controlled. I hope we don't have the same disorganization as with the nursing homes!

The United States is on the road to vaccine efficacy and dispensing at warp speed! This will lead us to herd immunity.

"Freedom is not free there is a price for you and for me."

— *Dianne Andrews*

TIDBITS AND LAGNIAPPE

Who funded the IHME?

IHME's largest donor was the Bill and Melinda Gates Foundation in 2017, gifting a $279 million grant to the institute, after 10 years earlier donating $105 million for its founding. Three years earlier, $210 million was donated from the foundation for a new building to house the IHME and the Department of Global Health, also funded by Gates. Both donations were the largest grants to the University of Washington.

There is so much inconsistency of in person school openings vs. remote learning. This subject is another book to investigate why not. In California the governor opened private in person learning so his kids could attend in person it seems. I wander if SARS-COV2 can tell more expensive school tuitions to spread. This virus is smarter than we know! One resource you may want to look at for more information www.edsource.org

China and Russia both claim to already have vaccines. Some believe they are working together.

The United States is working with seven companies after interviewing 100 pharma companies in February: Pfizer BioNTech- 2 dose mRNA vaccine, Moderna -2 dose mRNA. All other candidates seem to be one dose vector technology's- AstraZeneca with Oxford University, and J&J, GSK, Sanofi, Merck. In October, Pfizer has even begun manufacturing, with 700,000 doses made, seeking Emergency Use Authorization in the United States in November. Then FDA approval. Both were received after the UK approval and administered the first vaccine in the world on an elderly patient.

Per the CDC, preliminary fatality rates in the United States are as follows: Ages: 85+: 27 percent, 65–84: 3–11 percent, 55–64: 1–3 percent, 20–54: <1 percent. As you can see, for the school aged, it is very small, less than the flu. Experts believe it will take a few years to understand the true mortality rate. Compared to the flu, it is lower in younger persons.

In Louisiana, 75 percent of the deaths this summer during the peak were people over 75 years of age with multiple co-morbidities, mostly minorities.

Do lockdowns work? Items to consider are economic losses; psychological losses; deaths; the closure of houses of worship; non family funerals; suicide increases; delayed surgeries, lack of needed tests, including colon, mammograms; domestic violence increases; virtual prom graduations; and remote education issues. UP to 60% of restaurants that may never open again. Where science proves that only 1.5% of spread can be attributed to in house dining. Common sense is that they did not work well. Ask your mayors if you live in a city that is still mostly locked down, continuing to ruin lives. WHY did it become political, with many cities like Los Angeles, New York City, and New Orleans, to name just a few?

"It takes courage to make a decision, courage to take a risk, and courage to get your wish."

— *Dianne Andrews*

References/Sources

Lindsay Graham, Press Release on July 27, 2020, on PPE Manufactured in the United States, lgraham.gov

Kenneth Rapoza, Japan Ditches China in Multi-Billion Dollar Coronavirus Shakeout, Forbes, April 9, 2020

Department of Labor, Bureau of Labor Statistics.

Katy Grimes, Masks and California Buying Masks from China, October 13, 2020, www.Californiaglobe.com

In April 2020 PolitiFact wrote on this, also N95 mask depletion

Snopes.com on the PPE budget

SacBee.com on March 19 Governor Newsom

Seattle Times on January 25, 2017, info on Bill Gates

ON USNI News on Mercy and Comfort

Spectator TV, NYT on Operation Warp Speed

NY Post, October 8, 2020, COVID-19 Lockdowns Are a Risky Experiment—and One That Failed

BioSpace.com and National Geographics and NIH.com on phase 3 COVID-19 vaccine trials.

Buzz Feed News, July 24 on 9 Elite Scientist Tried to Warn against Lockdowns in March

The Verge on February 18, 2015. On solar panels in Buffalo, NY

Statista.com on deaths by country and state

Bristol Heard Courier, NYT on Governor Cuomo solar panel and ventilator supplies

Real Clear Politics on March 8, 2020, on Gov Cuomo on corona

PsychologyToday.com

Pulmotect.com on PUL-42

ProPublica.com on the CDC "accelerated policy" on lab testing

Census.gov

www.youtube.com/dianneandrewsshow

APPENDIX

PROCLAMATION

Proclamation on Suspension of Entry as Immigrants and Nonimmigrants of Persons who Pose a Risk of Transmitting 2019 Novel Coronavirus

Healthcare
Issued on: January 31, 2020
Share:
All News

The United States has confirmed cases of individuals who have a severe acute respiratory illness caused by a novel (new) coronavirus ("2019-nCoV") ("the virus") first detected in Wuhan, Hubei Province, People's Republic of China ("China"). The virus was discovered in China in December 2019. As of January 31, 2020, Chinese health officials have reported approximately 10,000 confirmed cases of 2019-nCoV in China, more than the number of confirmed cases of Severe Acute Respiratory Syndrome (SARS) during its 2003 outbreak. An additional 114 cases have been confirmed across 22 other countries; in several of these cases, the infected individuals had not visited China. More than 200 people have died from the virus, all in China.

Coronaviruses are a large family of viruses. Some cause illness in people, and others circulate among animals, including camels, cats, and bats. Animal coronaviruses are capable of evolving to infect people and subsequently spread through human-to-human transmission. This occurred with both Middle East Respiratory Syndrome and SARS. Many of the individuals with the earliest confirmed cases of 2019-nCoV in Wuhan, China, had a link to a large seafood and live animal market, suggesting animal-to-human transmission. Later, a growing number of infected individuals reportedly did not have exposure to animal markets, indicating human-to-human transmission. Chinese officials now report that sustained human-to-human transmission of the virus is occurring in China. Manifestations of severe disease have included severe pneumonia, acute respiratory distress syndrome, septic shock, and multi-organ failure.

Neighboring jurisdictions have taken swift action to protect their citizens by closing off travel between their territories and China. On January 30, 2020, the World Health Organization declared the 2019-nCoV outbreak a public health emergency of international concern.

Outbreaks of novel viral infections among people are always of public health concern, and older adults and people with underlying health conditions may be at increased risk. Public health experts are still learning about the severity of 2019-nCoV. An understanding of the key attributes of this novel virus, including its transmission dynamics, incubation period, and severity, is critical to assessing the risk it poses to the American public. Nonetheless, the Centers for Disease Control and Prevention (CDC) has determined that the virus presents a serious public health threat.

The CDC is closely monitoring the situation in the United States; is conducting enhanced entry screening at five US airports, where the majority of travelers from Wuhan arrive; and is enhancing illness response capacity at the 20 ports of entry where CDC medical screening stations are located. The CDC is also supporting states in conducting contact investigations of confirmed 2019-nCoV cases identified within the United States. The CDC has confirmed that the virus has spread between two people in the United States, representing the first instance of person-to-person transmission of the virus within the United States. The CDC, along with state and local health departments, has limited resources, and the public health system could be overwhelmed if sustained human-to-human transmission of the virus occurred in the United States. Sustained human-to-human transmission has the potential to have cascading public health, economic, national security, and societal consequences.

During Fiscal Year 2019, an average of more than 14,000 people traveled to the United States from China each day, via both direct and indirect flights. The US Government is unable to effectively evaluate and monitor all of the travelers continuing to arrive from China. The potential for widespread transmission of the virus by infected individuals seeking to enter the United States threatens the security of our transportation system, infrastructure, and national security. Given the importance of protecting persons within the United States from the threat of this harmful communicable disease, I have determined it is in the interests of the United States to take action to restrict and suspend entry into the United States, as immigrants or nonimmigrants, of all aliens who were physically present within the People's Republic of China, excluding the Special Administrative Regions of Hong Kong and Macau, during the 14-day period preceding their entry or attempted entry into the United States. I have also determined that the United States should take all necessary and appropriate measures to facilitate orderly medical screening and, where appropriate, quarantine persons allowed to enter the United States who may have been exposed to this virus.

NOW, THEREFORE, I, DONALD J. TRUMP, President of the United States, by the authority vested in me by the Constitution and the laws of the United States of America, including sections 212(f) and 215(a) of the Immigration and Nationality Act (INA), 8 U.S.C. 1182(f) and 1185(a), and section 301 of title 3, United States Code, hereby find that the unrestricted entry into the United States of persons described in section 1 of this proclamation would, except as provided for in section 2 of this proclamation, be detrimental to the interests of the United States, and that their entry should be subject to certain restrictions, limitations, and exceptions. I therefore proclaim the following:

Section 1. Suspension and Limitation on Entry. The entry into the United States, as immigrants or nonimmigrants, of all aliens who were physically present within the People's Republic of China, excluding the Special Administrative Regions of Hong Kong and Macau, during the 14-day period preceding their entry or attempted entry into the United States is hereby suspended and limited subject to section 2 of this proclamation.

Sec. 2. Scope of Suspension and Limitation on Entry.

(a) Section 1 of this proclamation shall not apply to:

(i) any lawful permanent resident of the United States;

(ii) any alien who is the spouse of a US citizen or lawful permanent resident;

(iii) any alien who is the parent or legal guardian of a US citizen or lawful permanent resident, provided that the US citizen or lawful permanent resident is unmarried and under the age of 21;

(iv) any alien who is the sibling of a US citizen or lawful permanent resident, provided that both are unmarried and under the age of 21;

(v) any alien who is the child, foster child, or ward of a US citizen or lawful permanent resident, or who is a prospective adoptee seeking to enter the United States pursuant to the IR-4 or IH-4 visa classifications;

(vi) any alien traveling at the invitation of the US Government for a purpose related to containment or mitigation of the virus;

(vii) any alien traveling as a nonimmigrant under section 101(a)(15)(C) or (D) of the INA, 8 U.S.C. 1101(a)(15)(C) or (D), as a crewmember or any alien otherwise traveling to the United States as air or sea crew;

(viii) any alien seeking entry into or transiting the United States pursuant to an A-1, A-2, C-2, C-3 (as a foreign government official or immediate family member of an official), G-1, G-2, G-3, G-4, NATO-1 through NATO-4, or NATO-6 visa;

(ix) any alien whose entry would not pose a significant risk of introducing, transmitting, or spreading the virus, as determined by the CDC director, or his designee;

(x) any alien whose entry would further important US law enforcement objectives, as determined by the Secretary of State, the Secretary of Homeland Security, or their respective designees based on a recommendation of the Attorney General or his designee; or

(xi) any alien whose entry would be in the national interest, as determined by the Secretary of State, the Secretary of Homeland Security, or their designees.

(b) Nothing in this proclamation shall be construed to affect any individual's eligibility for asylum, withholding of removal, or protection under the regulations issued pursuant to the legislation implementing the Convention Against

Torture and Other Cruel, Inhuman, or Degrading Treatment or Punishment, consistent with the laws and regulations of the United States.

Sec. 3. Implementation and Enforcement. (a) The Secretary of State shall implement this proclamation as it applies to visas pursuant to such procedures as the Secretary of State, in consultation with the Secretary of Homeland Security, may establish. The Secretary of Homeland Security shall implement this proclamation as it applies to the entry of aliens pursuant to such procedures as the Secretary of Homeland Security, in consultation with the Secretary of State, may establish.

(b) Consistent with applicable law, the Secretary of State, the Secretary of Transportation, and the Secretary of Homeland Security shall ensure that any alien subject to this proclamation does not board an aircraft traveling to the United States.

(c) The Secretary of Homeland Security may establish standards and procedures to ensure the application and implementation of this proclamation at US seaports and in between all ports of entry.

(d) An alien who circumvents the application of this proclamation through fraud, willful misrepresentation of a material fact, or illegal entry shall be a priority for removal by the Department of Homeland Security.

Sec. 4. Orderly Medical Screening and Quarantine. The Secretary of Homeland Security shall take all necessary and appropriate steps to regulate the travel of persons and aircraft to the United States to facilitate the orderly medical screening and, where appropriate, quarantine persons who enter the United States and who may have been exposed to the virus. Such steps may include directing air carriers to restrict and regulate the boarding of such passengers on flights to the United States.

Sec. 5. Termination. This proclamation shall remain in effect until terminated by the President. The Secretary of Health and Human Services shall, as circumstances warrant and no more than 15 days after the date of this order and every 15 days thereafter, recommend that the President continue, modify, or terminate this proclamation.

Sec. 6. Effective Date. This proclamation is effective at 5:00 p.m. eastern standard time on February 2, 2020.

Sec. 7. Severability. It is the policy of the United States to enforce this proclamation to the maximum extent possible to advance the national security, public safety, and foreign policy interests of the United States. Accordingly:

(a) if any provision of this proclamation, or the application of any provision to any person or circumstance, is held to be invalid, the remainder of this proclamation and the application of its provisions to any other persons or circumstances shall not be affected thereby; and

(b) if any provision of this proclamation, or the application of any provision to any person or circumstance, is held to be invalid because of the lack of certain procedural requirements, the relevant executive branch officials shall implement those procedural requirements to conform with existing law and with any applicable court orders.

Sec. 8. General Provisions. (a) Nothing in this proclamation shall be construed to impair or otherwise affect:

(i) the authority granted by law to an executive department or agency, or the head thereof; or

(ii) the functions of the Director of the Office of Management and Budget relating to budgetary, administrative, or legislative proposals.

(b) This proclamation shall be implemented consistent with applicable law and subject to the availability of appropriations.

(c) This proclamation is not intended to, and does not, create any right or benefit, substantive or procedural, enforceable at law or in equity by any party against the United States, its departments, agencies, or entities, its officers, employees, or agents, or any other person.

IN WITNESS WHEREOF, I have hereunto set my hand this thirty-first day of January, in the year of our Lord two thousand twenty, and of the Independence of the United States of America the two hundred and forty-fourth.

DONALD J. TRUMP

The White House

"We all should leave a path of goodness for others to follow."

Dianne Andrews, MBA, PhD started her professional career at IBM at 19 years old with a BS in mathematics, as a computer programmer on the Space Shuttle. She was promoted to several locations including Atlanta, Houston and New York in executive management prior to leaving to care for her mother in Louisiana. Armed with the BEST management training, experience, and an entrepreneurial drive she started and ran a beauty line with a boutique, 3 home health agencies and 6 sleep disorder clinics. She is admittedly a perfectionist and workaholic yet humble and compassionate. Dianne started writing fiction to relieve stress. This is her 5th book- 2 fiction and 3 nonfiction including one with 85 motivational quotes. She produces Dianne Andrews, In Black & White, a regional television talk show and is a transformational speaker while working on her 6th book, a nonfiction. She says most of all she is a "truth-seeker."

Speaking Engagements and Book Sales
225-933-0224 • gumboheart0@gmail.com
Please Subscribe www.youtube.com/dianneandrewsshow